Arrivals and Departures

Navigating Between Life and Death

Charles E. Cravey

In His Steps Publishing

Copyright © 2025 by Charles Edward Cravey

All rights reserved.

No portion of this book may be reproduced in any form without written permission from the publisher or author, except as permitted by U.S. copyright law.

All scripture references are taken from the King James Version of the Holy Bible.

ISBN: 978-1-58535-053-7

ISBN: 978-1-58535-054-4

Library of Congress Catalog Number: 2025905929

Published in the United States of America by

IN HIS STEPS PUBLISHING, Statesboro, Georgia

Table of Contents

Dedication	V
Introduction	VII
1. Letter to my 10-year Old Self	1
2. A Life Lived	3
3. Beginnings and Endings	9
4. Arrivals and Departures	25
5. The Threshold of Existence	30
6. In the Valley of Dry Bones	41
7. First Breath as Viewed by Other Cultures	47
8. Key Arrivals that Shape Childhood	61
9. Letter to my 20-year-old Self	75
10. Midlife - The Long Station Stop	78

11.	Letter to my 50-year-old Self	94
12.	Later Years - A Time of Perspective	97
13.	Letter to my Future Self	110
14.	Beyond the Final Departure	113
15.	What Happens When Aging	119
Epilogue		121

Dedication

For those who are no longer here

yet remain in every step of my journey.

This book carries your light.

Introduction

Life is a journey defined by its arrivals and departures. From the first breath we draw to the final sigh we release, we navigate a path marked by moments of profound beginnings, inevitable endings, and the transitions that bridge the two.

This book is an invitation to explore these pivotal moments with courage and curiosity. It is not merely about understanding life and death as concepts but about finding meaning in the spaces between them. Through reflective storytelling, universal truths, and heartfelt insights, *Arrivals and Departures* encourages readers to embrace both the joy and sorrow of existence.

Whether you are seeking solace, facing loss, or simply pondering the mysteries of life, may this book serve as a companion on your journey—a reminder that even in the face of departure, there is beauty to be found in the journey itself.

The Rev. Dr. Charles E. Cravey, March 2025

1

Letter to my 10-year Old Self

Dear Ten-year-old Me,

Greetings, dear one. In this moment, your universe sparkles with awe, yet shadows of uncertainty linger. Embrace this uncertainty—life is a grand quest, and each twist and turn will sculpt you into something truly remarkable.

Continue to nurture your curiosity; your questions and vivid imagination are your extraordinary gifts. Never allow others to dull your brilliance or convince you that your dreams are too vast. One day, you shall glance back and see that those grand dreams were merely the beginning of your journey. And remember, fret not over trivial matters—schoolyard squabbles, a missed test question, or that awkward moment in the school play will not define your essence.

Cherish your generous heart—tend to it lovingly. Cling to that kindness, even when the world seems daunting. It will propel you further than you can fathom.

With Love,
Your 74-Year-Old Self

2

A Life Lived

This June, I shall celebrate the milestone of seventy-four years. Throughout this journey, I have witnessed remarkable events that have eluded the eyes of other generations. Television allowed us to observe these moments, first in monochrome, and then in vibrant color. Each technological advancement bridged the gap between distant lands, bringing the world closer together. From the first moon landing, a spectacle that ignited the imagination of millions, to the fall of the Berlin Wall, a symbol of unity and hope for a better future, these events have left indelible marks in my memory.

As I reflect on these milestones, I am reminded of the resilience and innovation that define the human spirit. The internet further transformed our lives, connecting us in ways we never thought possible. The internet's arrival opened doors to knowledge and understanding, fostering a global community that shared ideas and cultures with a click.

In these seventy-four years, I've learned the importance of cherishing each moment, embracing change, and remaining curious. The world continues to develop, and as I celebrate this milestone, I look forward to witnessing the wonders yet to come, with gratitude for the journey so far and excitement for the adventures that lie ahead.

Allow me to weave a tapestry of the significant moments that have graced my life, bestowing clarity upon my reflections.

In 1953, Watson and Crick unveiled the very fabric of life itself by discovering the structure of DNA, a revelation that would transform medicine and empower justice to trace and apprehend those who left their marks.

In 1955, Rosa Parks ignited a firestorm of change in America with her courageous stand during the Montgomery Bus Boycott, a landmark event in the U.S. Civil Rights Movement.

Then, in 1957, the Soviet Union launched Sputnik 1, heralding the dawn of the Space Age, and captivating the imagination of the globe.

As the 1960s unfurled, I bore witness to the March on Washington, captivated by Dr. Martin Luther King, Jr.'s iconic "I Have a Dream" speech. His words, powerful and poignant, challenged America to confront the deep-seated inequities between black and white. Tragically, they took him from us in Memphis, Tennessee, a moment that indelibly marked my spirit.

In 1969, I watched in awe on a black-and-white screen as humans set foot on the Moon during the historic Apollo 11 mission.

The invention of email in 1971 transformed communication for both businesses and individuals, coinciding with my high school graduation—a momentous milestone for someone who had long harbored a disdain for academia!

The cultural phenomenon of Star Wars burst onto the scene in 1977, soon followed by Star Trek, captivating fans with epic tales of the cosmos!

In 1989, the Berlin Wall fell, symbolizing the twilight of the Cold War. The 1980s also ushered in the age of personal computers, with pioneers like Apple and IBM leading the charge. I fondly recall my first computer, a Gateway, which made my typing infinitely swifter and more efficient than my old IBM typewriter.

In 1991, researchers unveiled the World Wide Web to the public, and in 1997, scientists cloned Dolly the sheep—one could only wonder what marvels lay ahead, even the cloning of humans?

The harrowing tragedy of 9/11 reshaped global politics and security, as we watched in horror as the Twin Towers fell to the ruthless attacks of foreigners in hijacked jetliners. Our collective vow became "Never Again!"

In 2007, the iPhone emerged, marking the dawn of the smartphone era. I still recall the days of running to a neighbor's home for any urgent calls as a child and, later, a teenager.

By 2012, the Curiosity Rover touched down on Mars, propelling planetary exploration into new realms. In 2019, scientists captured the first image of a black hole; its implications still elude my understanding.

The year 2020 brought forth the COVID-19 pandemic, altering life as we knew it, presenting unprecedented challenges and sparking innovations. We donned masks and grappled with the unsettling notion that the virus had origins linked to monkeys in China. In those harrowing early days, countless people lost their lives.

Today, we stand at the precipice of remarkable advancements in AI (artificial intelligence), climate initiatives, and profound global shifts that define this current decade.

All of this, encapsulated within a mere seventy-four years.

These reflections serve not only as a testament to the passage of time but also as a celebration of the human capacity for growth and adaptation. Each of these significant moments has, in its own way, shaped the world and contributed to the tapestry of my life experiences.

As we continue to forge ahead, I find solace in knowing that the future holds boundless potential, driven by the same curiosity and determination that has propelled us thus far. The stories we share, the lessons we learn, and the connections we build will continue to guide us through the ever-developing landscape of our shared existence.

Looking back, I am filled with gratitude for the journey and the opportunity to have witnessed such transformative times. And as I stand on the brink of new beginnings, I remain hopeful and eager for what lies ahead, ready to embrace the unknown and cherish every moment as it unfolds.

3

Beginnings and Endings

BEGINNINGS

It was mid-morning when I stood beside my radiant wife in the sacred space of the delivery room. She was nine centimeters dilated on the cusp of bringing our first child into the world. Though we were still mere youths, a thrill coursed through us as we awaited our daughter's grand debut into a realm filled with vibrant lights and joyful cacophony. What visage would she bear? How might she measure in this world? Would she, in time, mend our hearts or inspire us with feats of wonder? The questions swirled in our minds, each one a testament to the boundless potential and mystery that lay ahead. Palpable anticipation and a sense of magic filled the room as the nurses moved with practiced ease, their gentle encouragement and warm smiles offering comfort.

In those moments, time seemed to stretch and compress all at once, each second both eternal and fleeting. My wife's hand gripped mine tightly, her strength and determination shining through, and I marveled at her courage and resilience. Her face, a mixture of concentration and serenity, was a portrait of grace and beauty.

With each contraction, we drew closer to the moment that would change our lives forever. The world outside faded away, leaving only this sacred space, this shared journey into the unknown. And then, with a final push and a symphony of emotion, our daughter arrived, her first cries echoing in the room, a melody of new beginnings.

She was perfect, tiny, and incredible, with a delicate face and eyes that held the universe within them. Her beauty instantly captivated us. As I looked at our daughter, I knew we stood at the threshold of a beautiful adventure, one that would be filled with laughter, challenges, and endless moments of wonder.

The nurse tenderly cleaned her, swaddled her in a cozy blanket, and gently placed her upon my wife's chest for our eager eyes to behold. Oh, the joy that enveloped us! Elated beyond measure, we gazed in wonder at this miraculous gift of life. For nine long months, we had eagerly awaited her arrival. Renee, my beloved, endured morning sickness, backaches, and dietary challenges, all while carrying our daughter. Together, we immersed ourselves in Lamaze classes, preparing for the momentous occasion. Our lives swirled with activity as we readied ourselves for this magnificent transformation awaiting us.

In that moment, all the trials and preparations seemed to fade away, replaced by a profound sense of peace and fulfillment. Our hearts synchronized with the gentle rise and fall of her tiny breaths, each one a testament to the miracle of life. As we whispered her name, our voices filled with tenderness and awe, she opened her eyes as if acknowledging her new world and the love that surrounded her.

The room seemed to glow with a soft warmth, the kind that only comes from newfound love and dreams yet to be realized. We knew that this was just the beginning, a first chapter in a story we would continue to write together as a family. Our journey was no longer just our own, but one shared with this precious new life, full of promise and potential.

A tender-hearted nurse inquired if I wished to bestow upon our daughter her inaugural bath, and my heart leaped at the chance. After gently cleansing her and lovingly enveloping her in a cozy blanket, the nurse nestled her into an incubator and whisked her away to the nursery for vigilant monitoring. Once our room was ready, they brought her back, cradled in her petite bed, and rolled it lovingly beside my wife.

As the day unfolded, we marveled at her smallest movements, her tiny fingers instinctively curling around ours, anchoring us to the present. We spoke of hopes and dreams, of the adventures we would embark on, of the lessons we would learn and teach. In that room, with the world beyond the walls momentarily forgotten, we found ourselves enveloped in a bubble of love and gratitude, ready to embrace whatever the future held.

The hours seemed to pass in a gentle haze, each moment a precious gem to be cherished. Family and friends visited, their faces lighting up with joy as they met the newest member of our family. Their congratulations and well-wishes filled the room, adding to the warmth and happiness that enveloped us.

We took turns holding her, our hearts swelling with pride and wonder with each little coo and sigh. The immense love inspired by such a small person left us marveling. We exchanged stories of childhood and parenthood, our laughter ringing out as we offered advice—some practical, some humorous, all given with love.

As the evening sun cast a golden glow through the window, we reflected on how much our lives had changed in just a single day. The future felt like an unwritten book, its pages waiting to be filled with memories and milestones. We knew there would be challenges ahead, sleepless nights and worries, but there would also be countless moments of joy and discovery, each one a testament to the incredible journey of parenthood.

In those muted moments, as we watched her sleeping peacefully, we felt a profound sense of gratitude—for each other, for our daughter, and for the opportunity to nurture and guide her as she grew. It was a journey we were eager to embark upon, hand in hand, heart in heart, bound by love and the shared dream of a bright and beautiful future together.

Only four years hence, we would embrace another cherished soul, a radiant baby boy. Our family blossomed, entwining us in extra responsibilities. Once more, we would joyfully welcome our little one into our hearts and home, transforming our lives forever.

We greeted his arrival with the same sense of awe and wonder that had enveloped us with our firstborn. This time, however, there was a familiar rhythm to the chaos, a seasoned confidence that comes from experience. Our daughter, now a spirited toddler, greeted her new sibling with curiosity and excitement, her giggles filling the room as she peeked into the bassinet to catch her first glimpse of her baby brother.

Our home, once a sanctuary of calm, now buzzed with the vibrant energy of a growing family. The days were a delightful whirlwind of laughter and learning as we navigated the joys and challenges of raising two young children. Our hearts expanded with each shared moment, from the tender sibling bonds forming between the two to the small milestones that marked their journeys.

We found joy in the simple things—morning cuddles, bedtime stories, and spontaneous dance parties in the living room. Each day brought fresh adventures, as our children explored the world around them with wide-eyed wonder. Their laughter was a melody that filled our home, a constant reminder of the beauty and magic that life holds.

As we embraced this new chapter, we cherished the opportunity to watch our children grow, to nurture their dreams, and to guide them as they discovered their own paths. Our family was a tapestry of love, woven together with moments of joy, resilience, and boundless affection.

With every bedtime lullaby and whispered goodnight, we knew that these days, though often exhausting, were fleeting. We were determined to savor each moment, to hold on to the precious memories that would one day become the stories we would share around the table, our hearts full of gratitude for the family we had become.

ENDINGS

I have just spent time with my cherished friend, who lies in a hospital bed, drifting in and out of delirium. Each moment, he battles the fragile thread of life. Yet, I find a sliver of gratitude for Alzheimer's, for it shields him from the full weight of the world unfolding around him. His eyes, though often clouded, occasionally spark with recognition, evoking memories of laughter and shared adventures. In those fleeting moments, I am reminded of the enduring spirit that still lives within him, untouched by the passage of time. As I sit by his side, I hold his hand, offering comfort and companionship, hoping he can feel the warmth of our friendship, even amidst the haze of his mind. A urinary tract infection had hampered his recovery and caused harm.

The hospital room, with its stark white walls and the constant hum of machines, becomes a sanctuary where love and memories are the balm against the harsh realities we face. I find solace in the minor victories: a smile, a squeeze of the hand, or a word spoken with clarity. These brief moments remind me of the bond we share, and I cherish them.

In those cherished moments of the past, we soared together, ascendant above the clouds, embarking on journeys to enchanting realms such as Spain, France, Central and South America, and the Caribbean, all in the noble pursuit of aiding our fellow believers. In snug tiny houses woven from straw or tarpaper, we nestled together in shared slumber. A medley of dishes—their names lost to time—adorned our tables as we intertwined our lives with countless kindred spirits whose memories linger like whispers in the breeze. I ponder if he still holds them close in his heart. In those rare moments of clarity, he revisits the tapestry of our shared history, feeling the warmth of camaraderie and the joy of those bygone days. The faces and laughter of kindred spirits etched deep within his soul serve as gentle reminders of a life richly lived. Even as the years have blurred the edges of those memories, the essence of love and connection remains, a muted flame that refuses to be extinguished.

Amidst the echoes of our past adventures, I hope he can feel those who care for him. It is in these muted reflections I realize the true power of our shared journey: the ability to transcend the boundaries of time and space, to touch the heart, and to find comfort in the simple, enduring truth of friendship.

At eighty-five, he must grasp the delicate truth that life is a fleeting wisp, a mere whisper carried away by the wind. This book weaves the journey of the spirit and the quest to uncover our origins into its very fabric.

As I sit by his side, I am reminded of the profound beauty in the transient nature of our existence. Each moment we have shared is a precious thread in the tapestry of our lives, binding us in ways that transcend the physical. In this muted space, I ponder the mysteries of our origins, the paths we've walked, and the lessons learned along the way. It is a journey filled with wonder and discovery, where the heart leads and the spirit follows.

The stories of our past, rich with adventure and purpose, are more than just memories; they are a testament to the love and resilience that define us. As I hold his hand, I feel an overwhelming sense of gratitude for the time we've had together, for the lessons imparted and the wisdom gained. Our shared history is a beacon of light, guiding us through the uncertainty of what lies ahead.

In these moments, I am reminded that while life may be fleeting, the bonds we forge are eternal. They live on in the hearts of those we touch, a legacy of love and friendship that endures beyond the boundaries of time. And so, as I sit with him, I find comfort in knowing that our journey, though nearing its end, has been one of profound meaning and beauty.

Between birth and death, in that short dash, lies the very essence of who we are. It is within this fleeting moment that we are born, blossom, grow, embrace the tapestry of life, and fade away. Far grander than our individual selves is this journey. It encompasses the souls we invite into our world and the adventures that captivate our hearts. Together, these elements weave a vibrant tapestry that defines our essence and shapes our destinies. The choices we embrace become threads in this intricate design, for in a sense, we craft our own tapestry from the decisions we've woven.

Each choice, each encounter, adds color and depth, and while some threads may be frayed by time, others remain strong and bright, reminding us of the moments that truly matter. It is in these choices that we find meaning, allowing us to reflect on what we have given and received, the love we have shared, and the lives we have touched.

As I sit beside my dear friend, I am reminded of the beauty in our shared tapestry—a masterpiece of laughter, tears, triumphs, and trials. This tapestry is not just a reflection of our lives, but a testament to the enduring power of connection and compassion. It is a reminder that even as time moves forward, the bonds we've formed remain unbroken, whispering softly of the love that has been and the love that will continue to be.

In the muted hospital room, I find peace knowing our lives intertwine profoundly. While we may not know what the future holds, the legacy of our friendship will endure, leaving an indelible mark on the world—a testament to the strength of the human spirit and the everlasting power of love.

I harbor no grand delusion that my cherished friend shall grace this world for another decade. His form is delicate, and the relentless hands of time have conspired against him in these twilight moments. He has journeyed far, toiled diligently, and waged the battles, emerging triumphant through his unwavering faith in the Divine he has proclaimed from sacred pulpits across the globe.

In this serene room, where time seems to slow and the world outside fades, I am left to reflect on the profound impact one life can have. We don't measure his legacy by years, but by the countless lives he touched with his kindness, wisdom, and unwavering devotion.

Every wrinkle on his face tells a story, a chapter of a life lived with purpose and passion. His eyes, though dimmed by age, still hold the spark of a man who has seen the beauty and sorrow of the world, yet remains steadfast in his belief in the goodness of humanity. As I sit beside him, I am reminded of the countless times he has inspired others to find the light within themselves, to strive for a higher purpose, and to live with compassion.

Though his body may be frail, his spirit remains indomitable, a beacon of hope and love that continues to glow. In his presence, I am reminded of the true meaning of strength—an inner resilience that transcends physical limitations and touches the hearts of those around him.

As we navigate these final chapters together, I find solace in knowing that our friendship is a testament to the enduring power of human connection. Shared experiences, laughter, and tears forged this bond, and it will remain a source of strength and comfort for both of us.

In the silent moments, I whisper my gratitude for his presence in my life and for the lessons he has imparted.

His journey may near its end, but the impact of his life will continue to ripple through the lives he has touched, a legacy of love, faith, and friendship.

I cherish those gentle moments when we sat in the shade together beneath the tractor shed, gazing out over the sprawling fields and the vibrant blueberry patch. We would ponder the intricate tapestry of life, reflecting on our existence and how, during those languid, sun-drenched days of summer, everything seemed to fall into place just perfectly. The scent of earth and ripe berries filled the air, a fragrant reminder of the simplicity and beauty of those times. We could lose ourselves in conversation for hours, weaving tales of dreams and aspirations, of the future we hoped to shape. The world seemed vast and full of possibilities, and yet, in those moments, it felt comforting.

As we sat there, the gentle hum of nature provided the perfect backdrop to our musings. The rustling leaves, the distant chirping of birds, and the occasional rustle of a gentle breeze through the tall grass seemed to echo the rhythm of our lives—unpredictable yet harmonious.

I have deeply etched these simple memories into my heart. They remind me of the importance of appreciating the present, to find joy in the insignificant things, and to cherish the connections that bind us. Even as time moves forward and life becomes more complex, these moments serve as an anchor, grounding me in the enduring truth that love, friendship, and shared experiences are the veritable treasures of life.

As I reminisce about those days, I am filled with gratitude for the journey we've shared and the countless memories that continue to warm my heart. They are a testament to the life we have lived, rich with meaning and underscored by the unbreakable bond of friendship.

As I leave, I whisper a silent promise to return, to be there for him in whatever way I can. I know that while the future may be uncertain, the love and friendship we have built will endure, providing strength and comfort in the days to come.

4

Arrivals and Departures

In the heart of Jackson-Hartsfield International Airport, nestled in Atlanta, Georgia—the busiest airport in the world—I find myself enveloped in the vibrant symphony of travelers ebbing and flowing; some embark on grand adventures, while others return to the warm embrace of home.

It has always stirred a disquiet within me to hear a steward proclaim, "And today, your **final destination is** …" Surely, the steward ought to say, "And today, your next destination will be…" Or, even more delightful, "Today, we shall arrive in the enchanting San Jose, Costa Rica."

Please, don't tell me that my "final destination" is where it all will end!

In the vibrant heart of Atlanta, a symphony of voices rises as travelers seek their cherished luggage, the portal to their destinations, or the welcoming gate for loved ones. It is a spectacle that captivates the senses. I watch a young mother valiantly maneuver a hefty suitcase while cradling her little one, battling time to reach her gate. Nearby, another wanderer, adorned with a guitar case slung around his neck, juggles a carry-on in one hand and a large suitcase in the other, embodying the spirit of adventure amidst the bustling throng.

Their paths briefly intersect, a shared glance and a knowing smile exchanged, as if acknowledging the unspoken camaraderie among travelers. It's a reminder of the countless stories unfolding simultaneously in this vast, transient space. The airport, with its intertwining narratives, becomes a microcosm of the world—a place where dreams take flight and new chapters begin.

As I continue to observe, I notice a pair of older travelers resting on a nearby bench, their fingers intertwined, whispering secrets of a lifetime spent together. Their presence exudes warmth and comfort, a testament to enduring love and companionship. It's moments like these that transform the mundane into something extraordinary, filling the airport with a palpable sense of humanity.

In this melting pot of emotions and experiences, the airport stands as a testament to the beauty of human connection, where eventual returns follow every departure, and every goodbye promises a future hello.

I'm embarking on a journey to the vibrant lands of Costa Rica, accompanied by a devoted team of missioners eager to lend our hands to a new church project. As we gather at the expansive windows, we watch in awe as planes arrive and depart, our hearts fluttering with anticipation. It's a truly wondrous setting, reflecting the beautiful chaos of life itself. Soon our plane will pull into the terminal, and we'll embark to that beautiful country I love so much.

Once more, I find myself at the edge of verdant banana groves, poised for the banana plane to descend and collect the precious boxed bananas, whisking them—and us—away from our work site and back to San Jose, where our journey home awaits. A lush grass field stretches between the groves, adorned with hands of bananas swaying gracefully. The small aircraft arrives to gather us, and off to San Jose we soar.

My life has been a tapestry woven with arrivals and departures. One might say they serve as both a profound metaphor and a tangible exploration of the various stages of existence. Each arrival heralds a new beginning, an opportunity to embrace the unknown and weave new threads into the fabric of my journey. Departures, conversely, signal the closing of chapters, but they also hold the promise of return, of coming full circle to where we started, enriched by experiences and memories gathered along the way.

In the spaces between arrivals and departures, I find the heart of my story. It's in the fleeting moments of connection—a shared smile with a fellow traveler, the comforting embrace of a loved one upon return, the anticipation of new horizons—that life unfurls in its most vivid hues. These moments remind me that each journey, whether grand or small, leaves an indelible mark on my soul, shaping who I am and who I am becoming.

As I stand poised to embark once more, I carry with me the lessons gleaned from past travels. The world, vast and varied, offers endless opportunities for discovery and growth. With each step, I remain open to the wonders that await, knowing that the tapestry of my life is ever developing, colored by the places I've seen and the people I've met.

The airport, in its bustling glory, serves as a poignant reminder of this cycle. It is here, amid the ebb and flow of travelers, that I am reminded of my place within the grand tapestry of humanity. And so, with a heart full of gratitude and a spirit ready for fresh adventures, I step forward, eager to see where the next departure will lead; hopefully not my **"final"** destination!

5

The Threshold of Existence

WHEN DOES LIFE BEGIN?

I suppose there lies little sagacity in contemplating the age-old riddle: which graced existence first—the chicken or the egg? It takes a chicken to bring forth an egg, does it not? Without these feathery beings, eggs would simply not be. It seems logical. Yet, a chicken must have emerged from somewhere at the dawn of time, mustn't it?

The genuine answer lies not in the linear progression of which came first, but in the wondrous cycle of life itself. Nature often defies simple explanations, weaving intricate patterns that challenge human logic. The chicken and the egg are partners in an eternal dance of creation, a reminder that beginnings and endings are not always as clear-cut as they seem. In pondering such mysteries, we find an opportunity to marvel at the complexity and beauty of life, recognizing that sometimes the questions themselves hold more value than the answers.

As we delve deeper into this enigmatic dance, we uncover the interconnectedness of all living things. Each element of nature plays its part in a grand symphony, where every note is essential to the harmony of existence. This eternal cycle invites us to embrace curiosity and wonder, to cherish the mysteries that remain unsolved, and to appreciate the simple yet profound truths that lie within the world. In the end, it is not the resolution of the riddle that matters, but the journey of discovery it inspires—a journey that enriches our understanding and appreciation of the intricate tapestry of life.

I do not possess all the answers to these intricate questions, yet I feel compelled to share the wisdom that seventy-four years of existence have bestowed upon me through extensive exploration, both philosophical and spiritual.

Strange though it may seem, let us embark on our journey at the very dawn of time. Yet can we truly begin if the whispers of THE beginning remain shrouded in mystery, save for the sacred verses of Moses in the Old Testament?

In those ancient texts, we find stories that have shaped the beliefs and cultures of countless generations. They tell of creation, of a universe spoken into existence with words of power and purpose. These sacred verses offer a glimpse into the profound mysteries that have captivated human imagination for millennia.

Even as we ponder these ancient tales, we must acknowledge the vast tapestry of creation myths from cultures around the world, each offering its own unique perspective on the origins of life and the universe. From the rich tapestries of Hindu cosmology to the intricate patterns of Native American storytelling, humanity's quest to understand the beginnings of existence is a universal endeavor.

As we explore these narratives, we find that they often reflect the values and wisdom of the cultures that birthed them. They serve as mirrors, reflecting our deepest fears, hopes, and dreams. They remind us that the quest for understanding is not just about seeking answers but about embracing the journey itself, with all its twists and turns.

In this exploration, we find a common thread: the recognition that life is a precious, interconnected web of relationships. Our journey through the creation stories invites us to see ourselves not as isolated beings, but as integral parts of a larger whole. This awareness calls us to live with reverence, to cherish the world and its inhabitants, and to nurture the delicate balance that sustains us all.

So, as we stand at the threshold of time's beginning, let us carry forward the wisdom of the past, allowing it to illuminate our path and guide us towards a future where understanding and compassion reign supreme.

FIRST BREATH

Let us embark upon a journey within the sacred pages of the King James Version of the Bible, specifically Chapter Two, Verse 7 of the book of Genesis. After the Creator fashioned the avian wonders of the sky and the majestic creatures of the earth, He turned His divine artistry toward man.

"And the Lord God formed man of the dust of the ground and breathed into his nostrils the breath of life; and **man became a living soul**." The first woman, Eve, would soon follow, crafted from Adam's very rib, a testament to the intertwining of their destinies.

Now, I invite you to ponder with me a singular aspect of this verse: "And **breathed** into his nostrils the breath of life." Can we not infer that without the divine spirit (Ruach) being exhaled into this mere assemblage of flesh and bone, Adam remained but a lifeless form? It certainly seems to suggest so, does it not?

This divine breath, this Ruach, is more than just the animation of the physical form—it is the spark that transforms matter into being, infusing it with consciousness and soul. It is a profound reminder of the sacred connection between the Creator and creation, illustrating that life itself is a gift given with intention and care.

God's *breathing* life into Adam signifies a moment of divine intimacy, bridging the boundary between the earthly and the ethereal. It speaks to the idea that life is not merely a biological process but a spiritual journey, one where each breath serves as a testament to our origins and our ongoing relationship with the divine.

This reflection invites us to consider the sacredness of our breath, the rhythm sustaining and connecting us to each other and the world. Each inhale and exhale become a meditation in our place in the universe, a reminder of our shared humanity and the divine spark that lives within us all.

In this contemplation, we find an invitation to live with intention, to honor the breath of life within us by nurturing the world we inhabit and the relationships we cherish. It is a call to recognize the sanctity of life in all its forms, to embrace kindness, compassion, and understanding as guiding principles in our shared journey.

Thus, as we ponder this verse, let us carry forward its wisdom, breathing life into our own actions and choices, and allowing the divine spirit to guide us towards a future filled with hope and harmony.

Humanity truly emerged when the divine "breath" of God infused life into being. In that sacred moment, as Moses recounts, Adam transformed into a "living soul." This profound notion offers ample material for both Pro-Choice and Pro-Life advocates seeking clarity on the pivotal question of when life genuinely begins.

Let us, if you please, revisit the whimsical egg analogy. An egg remains but a vessel until it yields its treasure, yes? It is only when the chick takes its inaugural breath, having valiantly pecked its way through the protective shell, that it transforms into a chicken!

This moment of emergence, when the chick breaks free and inhales its first breath, mirrors the profound transformation described in sacred texts—the transition from potential to actuality, from mere possibility to vibrant life. It is a beautiful metaphor for the awakening of consciousness and the beginning of an independent journey.

The humble egg, with its delicate yet resilient shell, serves as a reminder of the nurturing protection required for life to flourish. It symbolizes the care and patience necessary for growth, as well as the courage needed to step into the unknown. Just as the chick must muster its strength to break free, so, too, must we find the courage within ourselves to overcome obstacles and embrace new beginnings. Like a baby's dramatic, painful birth, our entrance into this world is equally dramatic and painful.

Reflecting on this analogy reminds us of life's cyclical nature and the interconnectedness of all living things. Each creature, from the smallest insect to the largest mammal, plays a role in the intricate web of existence, contributing to the balance and harmony of the natural world. This understanding encourages us to approach life with humility and gratitude, recognizing the value of every **breath** and every moment.

Contemplating the miraculous journey from egg to chick to chicken invites us to cherish life's unfolding in all its forms, to honor the process of becoming, and to celebrate the wonders of creation. In doing so, we cultivate a deeper appreciation for the miracle of life and the shared journey we all embark upon.

In the sacred tapestry of the Old Testament, the figure of Job, the steadfast servant of suffering, recognizes that the essence of life flows from the divine hand of God, and each breath we draw is a cherished gift from the Almighty. According to Job 33:4, "The spirit of God hath made me, and the breath of the Almighty hath given me life."

Once more, this sacred "breath" reminds us it infuses us with vitality. This profound acknowledgment of the divine breath highlights the intimate connection between humanity and the Creator, a bond that transcends the physical and touches the spiritual. It is a reminder that life is not merely a series of biological functions, but a sacred journey imbued with purpose and meaning.

In the story of Job, we witness a testament to resilience and faith, even amidst profound suffering. Job's unwavering trust in the divine plan, despite his trials, speaks to the strength derived from that sacred breath. It encourages us to find solace and hope, knowing that we are part of something greater, a divine narrative that weaves through the fabric of existence.

As we draw each breath, let us do so with gratitude and awareness, cherishing the life force that sustains us. May we use this gift to foster understanding, compassion, and love in our interactions with others, nurturing the world and its inhabitants. Embracing this perspective invites us to live in harmony with the universe, acknowledging the interconnectedness that binds us all.

Thus, in the spirit of Job's enduring faith and the divine breath that animates us, let us embark on our journey with courage and purpose, ever mindful of the blessings given to us and the responsibility we carry to honor them. May our lives reflect the divine grace that breathes life into us as we strive to create a future filled with hope, peace, and unity.

I vividly recall the instant my daughter took her inaugural breath in the delivery suite—a moment that shimmered with significance for my wife and me. As her cry pierced the air with a joyful squeal, we celebrated, for it heralded her existence. **That very breath is the essence of life**, nurturing us through our days. When it fades, so too does our existence. We are but vessels until the divine spirit breathes vitality into us, awakening us as "a living soul." In that moment, the miracle of creation unfolded before our eyes, a testament to the wonder and fragility of life. We felt an overwhelming sense of awe and gratitude; time itself seemed to pause in honor of this new life's arrival. Her tiny fingers grasped the air, her eyes blinked open to the world, and in that instant, we understood the profound connection between the past, present, and future.

This sacred breath, shared by all living beings, connects us to generations before and those yet to come. It's a reminder of the cycle of life, where each beginning is both a continuation and a new chapter. As parents, we felt an immense responsibility to nurture and guide her, to teach her the values of kindness, love, and understanding, and to help her find her place in the world.

Every breath she takes is a reminder of the beauty and potential within her, a reflection of the divine spark that animates us all. It's a call to cherish each moment, to live fully and intentionally, and to embrace the journey of life with open hearts and minds. Witnessing her first breath reminded us of our shared humanity, the preciousness of life, and the importance of fostering a world where every soul can thrive.

As we hold her close, we feel hopeful for the future and inspired to create a legacy of compassion and wisdom that she can continue. In this way, the simple act of breathing becomes a powerful symbol of life's continuity and the enduring spirit of love that binds us all together.

The divine essence of God, as inscribed in Genesis 1, hovered over the waters, bestowing life upon all of creation. This sacred spirit continues to stir within us today, affirming our very existence. Think on these thoughts as you breathe the breath of life every moment. It is the very essence of God.

6

In the Valley of Dry Bones

Let us delve deeper into the quest for understanding when life truly begins. The **Valley of Dry Bones** story in Ezekiel 37 illuminates the vision, meaning, and significance of the chapter.

Ezekiel, a revered prophet amidst the shadows of Babylonian exile, encounters a divine vision. He stands in a boundless valley, where dry, lifeless bones lie scattered, remnants of a long-forgotten past. These skeletal remains, having succumbed to time's relentless embrace years or decades ago, paint a scene both surreal and haunting. As he gazes across this desolate expanse, a profound sense of hopelessness envelops Ezekiel's heart, echoing the sorrow of the valley's silent whispers.

Ezekiel's profound journey offers a wealth of symbolism and invaluable lessons. We understand the bones to embody the nation of Israel, a land that has endured devastation, exile, and a profound loss of hope. This vision unfolds as a beacon of restoration and renewed hope.

Amid this desolation, a voice calls out to Ezekiel, instructing him to prophesy over the bones. As he speaks the words of life, a miraculous transformation begins. The bones start to rattle and shift, drawing together with a sense of purpose. Tendons and flesh gradually cover them, breathing new life into what was once lifeless. This powerful imagery serves as a reminder that, even in despair, renewal is possible.

The vision seeks to reassure the people of Israel that their current struggles are not their last story. Just as the bones revive, so too can a nation rejuvenate its spirit and future. It emphasizes the enduring power of faith and the belief that, with divine intervention, revival is always within reach. Collective hope and unwavering belief in a brighter future create the strength and unity symbolized by the bones rising to form a vast, living army.

Ezekiel's vision transcends the confines of its historical backdrop, imparting a timeless message of hope and resilience. It beckons us to peer beyond the veil of despair and embrace the potential for transformation, regardless of how dire the circumstances may seem.

God commanded Ezekiel to prophesy life into the bones, an act that reveals divine power to restore what appears irreparably shattered. The bones uniting, sinews weaving, and flesh enveloping them epitomize the essence of spiritual revival. Just as the dry bones signify, Israel too shall experience renewal and a heartfelt return to God.

When the breath of God infuses those lifeless forms, a miraculous transformation unfolds. Before this divine breath, Israel existed in the physical realm, yet remained spiritually disconnected from God. As the **breath** flows in, the bones awaken to vibrant life, symbolizing God's promise to reinvigorate Israel and guide them back to their homeland. This breath of life represents more than mere physical revival; it signifies a profound spiritual awakening, a reawakening of faith and purpose. The vision underscores the idea that no situation is beyond redemption and that even the most desolate moments can be the catalyst for profound change and renewal.

In our own lives, the story of the Valley of Dry Bones resonates as a metaphor for overcoming adversity. It encourages us to find strength in community and faith during times of personal exile or spiritual drought. Challenges that leave us feeling fragmented or hopeless remind us that transformation is possible, and that we, too, can rise from our valleys with renewed vigor and purpose.

Ezekiel's vision offers a powerful testament to the resilience of the human spirit and the boundless potential for rebirth. It invites us to trust in the unseen possibilities and to have faith that, with the right nurturing and belief, we can rebuild and emerge stronger, unified, and revitalized.

Some biblical scholars perceive this vision as a tangible resurrection, an omen of God's dominion over the realms of life and death. Others interpret it as a rich metaphor for Israel's revival from the shackles of captivity. The valley of dry bones symbolizes any desolate and despair-laden plight—be it personal tribulations, societal dilemmas, or spiritual crises. It is precisely in these shadowy times that God beckons us to prophesy life and hope into our tribulations.

This tale serves as a poignant reminder that even amidst our most profound darkness, God has the power to infuse vitality into what appears irreparable. It imparts lessons on divine intervention, rejuvenation, and the essence of hope. In our spiritually parched moments, it is God's word and Spirit that breathes life anew within us. Through this lens, the Valley of Dry Bones becomes a powerful allegory, urging us to look beyond our immediate struggles and to trust in the transformative power of faith. It reassures us that no matter how dire our circumstances may seem, there is a divine promise of renewal and restoration waiting to be fulfilled.

In contemporary times, this message holds significant relevance. Challenges that test our resilience and faith—personal hardships or broader societal issues—often confront us. The story inspires us to look actively for ways to improve ourselves and to share optimism and hope with others. It reminds us that, just as Ezekiel was called to prophesy over the bones, we, too, are called to be agents of change and positivity in our world.

The vision of the Valley of Dry Bones invites us to embrace a mindset of hopefulness and to recognize the endless possibilities for growth and renewal. It teaches us that with faith, perseverance, and a belief in the divine potential for change, we can overcome even the most formidable obstacles and emerge stronger, more unified, and spiritually enriched.

7

First Breath as Viewed by Other Cultures

In the rich tapestry of **Hinduism**, the inaugural breath holds profound significance. It marks the sacred instant when the soul, known as Atman, graces the vessel of the body. This act of breathing weaves a bond between the individual and the divine life force, Prana. The Garbhadhana Samskara ritual, celebrated during the sacred journey of pregnancy, underscores the vital essence of conception and the soul's passage into the developing fetus. Thus, the first breath emerges as a powerful emblem of the soul's voyage into the realm of the physical.

This understanding imbues the rituals and traditions surrounding birth in Hindu culture with deep spiritual meaning. The welcoming of a new life is not merely a biological event, but a celebration of the soul's entry into a new chapter of existence. Each breath thereafter is a part of the divine dance of creation, a testament to the interconnectedness of all beings within the universe.

The teachings of Hinduism remind us that every breath carries the potential for spiritual awakening, encouraging mindfulness and reverence for life. As the child grows, parents often embrace rituals such as the Namakarana, or naming ceremony, which further sanctifies the child's identity and place within the cosmic order. Thus, we celebrate the journey of life, from the very first breath, as a sacred pilgrimage, rich with opportunities for growth, learning, and spiritual fulfillment.

In the realm of **Buddhism**, beliefs may diverge, yet certain traditions illuminate the path of breath awareness. Meditation practices frequently center on the gentle flow of breath, serving as a vessel to nurture mindfulness and inner tranquility. Although Buddhism does not explicitly speak to the inaugural breath of life, the principle of impermanence beautifully highlights the fleeting essence of existence, encompassing each breath we draw. In this context, the breath becomes a focal point for meditation, guiding practitioners to remain present and attentive to the current moment. This practice, known as Anapanasati, or mindfulness of breathing, is a key component of Buddhist meditation. It encourages individuals to observe their breath, noticing its natural rhythm and the sensations it brings, fostering a sense of peace and clarity.

Through this meditative discipline, one learns to let go of attachments and mental clutter, cultivating a deeper understanding of the self and the nature of reality. Each breath is an opportunity to renew awareness and embrace the simplicity of being, highlighting the interconnectedness of all life.

The act of breathing is a bridge between the body and mind, harmonizing the physical and spiritual aspects of existence. Focusing on their breath allows practitioners to achieve equanimity, observing thoughts and emotions without judgment, thus fostering greater insight and compassion.

Thus, while the inaugural breath may not hold the same ceremonial significance, the ongoing awareness of breath in Buddhism underscores a profound respect for life and the present moment, guiding individuals on their journey toward enlightenment and spiritual awakening.

In the sacred tapestry of Judaism, Jews revere the breath as a divine endowment. People believe the Neshamah, symbolizing both breath and soul, takes residence within the body at birth. This inaugural breath marks the soul's graceful embodiment. On the eighth day following birth, the Brit Milah, a profound circumcision ceremony for boys, unfolds, binding the child to the ancient covenant. Thus, the breath of life weaves its essential thread into this sacred rite.

This act reaffirms the child's place within the Jewish community and their connection to the lineage and traditions passed down through generations. The breath, in this context, is not just a sign of life, but also a symbol of continuity, faith, and divine promise.

Beyond these ancient rituals, the breath continues to play a vital role in Jewish spiritual practices. Prayer and meditation often involve focused breathing, creating a rhythm that aligns the mind and spirit with sacred intentions. The breath becomes a tool for introspection and connection to the divine, allowing individuals to quiet their minds and open their hearts.

The breath is present in the recitation of sacred texts and prayers, infusing them with life and sincerity. The breath carries each uttered word, transforming it into a living testament of faith. This practice underscores the belief that every breath is a gift and an opportunity to engage with one's spiritual path, nurturing a relationship with the divine.

In this way, the breath in Judaism is more than a physiological necessity; it is an integral part of spiritual expression and identity, a reminder of the divine presence in everyday life and a call to live with purpose and gratitude.

In **Islam**, the first breath holds profound significance, yet it is not the central focus. The Quran beautifully recognizes God as the divine bestower of life and breath. Seven days after the birth, people hold an Aqiqah ceremony to honor the newborn's arrival, sacrificing an animal in celebration. This sacred act embodies gratitude for the gift of life and the sustenance it brings.

The Aqiqah gives thanks and shares blessings with the community, as people often distribute the sacrificed meat among family, friends, and those in need. This gesture reflects the values of generosity and compassion, emphasizing the interconnectedness and responsibility individuals have toward one another.

Besides the Aqiqah, the Islamic tradition involves whispering the Adhan, or call to prayer, into the newborn's ear shortly after birth. This act introduces the child to the core tenets of faith and serves as a gentle reminder of the divine presence that will guide them throughout their life. Therefore, these first words give the child spiritual significance, establishing a foundation for a life of faith and devotion.

The breath in Islam symbolizes the continuous presence of God's mercy and guidance. Mindful breathing in regular prayer and reflection encourages Muslims to connect spiritually and find tranquility. Each breath taken during prayer is an opportunity to seek closeness to God, to express gratitude, and to find peace within the rhythm of devotion.

In this way, while people may not celebrate the inaugural breath with specific rituals, they nonetheless cherish it as a precious gift from the Creator. The breath is a reminder of life's fragility and beauty, inspiring individuals to lead lives of purpose, kindness, and reverence for the divine.

In our **Native American Traditions**, a profound reverence for nature and the intricate web of interconnectedness flourishes. Breath embodies the sacred bond that unites humans, animals, and the environment. In smudging rituals, practitioners gently ignite sacred herbs, frequently weaving in prayers for cleansing and renewal, highlighting breath as a vital conduit for spiritual energy.

In many tribes, the act of breathing is a way to connect with the Great Spirit, the life force that animates all living things. Tribes celebrate this connection through various ceremonies and practices honoring the breath as a gift from the Creator.

For instance, during a Vision Quest, a rite of passage for many Native American cultures, individuals seek solitude in nature to pray and meditate, often focusing on their breath to gain insight and guidance. This sacred time allows them to tune into the rhythms of the earth, listening to the whispers of the wind and the songs of the birds, all of which are carried on the breath of life.

The breath is also integral to traditional healing practices, where healers may use breathwork to channel energy and restore balance within the body. This practice emphasizes the belief that breath carries the power to heal and transform, promoting harmony and well-being.

Storytelling, a cherished tradition in Native American cultures, relies on the breath to bring stories to life. Storytellers infuse each shared narrative with their breath, creating a living link between past and present and preserving ancestral wisdom for future generations.

In these ways, breath in Native American traditions is more than a mere act of respiration; it is a sacred force that binds individuals to their community, the natural world, and the spiritual realm. It reminds them of their duty to live in harmony with all creation, nurturing a profound sense of respect, gratitude, and responsibility.

In **Chinese** Culture, the ancient wisdom of traditional Chinese medicine celebrates the vital essence of breath (Qi or Chi) as the cornerstone of health and harmony. Practices such as Qigong dedicate themselves to the nurturing of this life force through the art of breath control. The inaugural breath taken at birth marks the beginning of the child's earthly odyssey, intertwining beautifully with the profound philosophy of Yin and Yang.

This balance of opposites, Yin and Yang, underscores the importance of harmony in all aspects of life, including one's physical and spiritual well-being. The breath, as a manifestation of Qi, is a conduit for maintaining this equilibrium, ensuring the free flow of energy throughout the body.

In the practice of Qigong, individuals engage in controlled breathing techniques, combined with gentle movements and meditation to cultivate and harmonize their Qi. This ancient discipline not only promotes physical health but also enhances mental clarity and emotional stability, embodying the holistic approach that is central to Chinese philosophy.

Encouraging children from an early age to develop breath awareness fosters a connection to their inner selves and the world around them. This mindfulness of breath serves as a foundation for lifelong health and spiritual growth, echoing the belief that true well-being arises from the seamless integration of mind, body, and spirit.

Martial arts deeply embed the role of breath, where practitioners learn to harness their Qi through precise breathing techniques, enhancing their strength, agility, and focus. This mastery of breath exemplifies the profound respect for the life force that permeates Chinese culture, highlighting its significance in achieving personal balance and harmony with the universe.

Thus, in Chinese culture, breath is much more than a physiological function; it is a vital thread that connects individuals to their heritage, their health, and the cosmic dance of Yin and Yang. It serves as a reminder of the interconnectedness of all things and the enduring quest for balance and harmony in every aspect of life.

African and Indigenous Beliefs perceive breath as a sacred conduit linking the earthly and the ethereal. Rituals weave together ancestral invocation and spirit communion, breathing life into their reverence. People hail the inaugural breath as the soul's grand entrance, with ceremonies beautifully honoring this age-old tradition.

In many African cultures, the breath is a bridge between the material world and the spiritual realm. People believe the wind's breath carries the spirits of ancestors, and ceremonies often include breath-carried offerings and prayers honoring these ancestral spirits.

Among various Indigenous communities, people similarly revere the breath as a force connecting individuals to their past, community, and the world. Rituals such as the pouring of libations involve the symbolic act of breathing out prayers and gratitude, acknowledging ancestors and the divine.

In addition, storytelling, a vital tradition within many African and Indigenous cultures, relies on the breath to animate and preserve the wisdom passed through generations. The act of sharing stories is a living testament to the enduring connection between the teller and their audience, each breath infusing the narrative with life and meaning.

The breath is integral to healing practices, where traditional healers might use breathwork to channel spiritual energy and restore harmony within individuals. This practice underscores the belief that breath holds the power to heal, transform, and connect, reinforcing the interconnectedness of all existence.

In these ways, breath in African and Indigenous beliefs is more than a mere physiological process; it is a sacred thread that binds individuals to their heritage, their environment, and the spiritual dimensions of life. It serves as a reminder of the sacredness of existence and the ongoing dialogue between the earthly and the celestial.

Our **Western Perspectives** frequently illuminate the physiological marvels of the first breath. Medical practitioners vigilantly observe the newborns' inaugural respiratory endeavors. Legal definitions of viability—such as the capacity to thrive beyond the womb—cast ripples in the ethical dialogues that encompass abortion and reproductive rights.

In the Western context, the focus on the first breath often combines scientific understanding with profound emotional significance. People celebrate a newborn's first breath as a miraculous transition from the sheltered life in the womb to independent existence in the world. This initial gasp symbolizes not only the beginning of life outside the womb but also represents the resilience and potential of human life.

From a medical standpoint, the first breath is critical as it marks the activation of the lungs and the start of the baby's independent breathing process. Healthcare professionals are keenly attentive, ensuring that the newborn's transition is smooth and that the lungs function effectively. This moment often brings a sense of relief and joy to the parents, as the cry of a newborn signifies not just the start of life but also a connection between parent and child, woven through shared breaths and experiences.

Beyond the medical and physiological, this moment resonates with profound emotional and philosophical implications in Western culture. It signifies a new beginning, full of possibilities and hope for the future. People often view the first breath as a metaphor for new opportunities and life's endless potential, inspiring parents and communities to nurture and support each unique individual's growth and development.

Psychologists and philosophers sometimes explore the breath as a symbol of life's cycles and the constant renewal of the self. This perspective invites a deeper reflection on existence and the continual process of becoming, encouraging individuals to embrace change and growth throughout their lives.

In this way, while the Western perspective may focus more heavily on the physiological aspects of the inaugural breath, it does not diminish the deeper significance it holds. It is a moment celebrated not just for its biological marvel but for its representation of life's promise and the shared human journey.

I have given you a tapestry of the world's beliefs surrounding the "first breath" and its profound significance.

It is now your sacred choice to embrace one, or weave together all, as your truth.

Whether you find resonance in the spiritual symbolism of Hinduism, the mindful awareness of Buddhism, the sacred traditions of Judaism, the communal celebrations of Islam, the harmonious philosophies of Chinese culture, the ancestral connections of African and Indigenous beliefs, or the scientific marvels of Western perspectives, the common thread uniting them all is the reverence for life and the unique journey that begins with that first breath.

This universal breath is a reminder of our shared humanity and the diverse ways we celebrate life's beginnings. It encourages us to reflect on the values and teachings that guide us, to appreciate the rich tapestry of beliefs that shape our understanding of existence, and to foster a sense of unity and respect for all cultures and their traditions.

In embracing this knowledge, please find your own path, one that honors the breath as a symbol of life's potential, a bridge between the physical and spiritual, and a testament to the interconnectedness of all beings. Let this understanding inspire you to live with mindfulness, gratitude, and a profound respect for the miraculous gift of life.

8

Key Arrivals that Shape Childhood

A child's first tentative steps, the sweet sound of their initial words, and the grand debut of the first day at school shimmer as pivotal milestones in the tapestry of early life, heralding a blossoming sense of independence and connection with the world. As families, we gather to celebrate and treasure these enchanting moments, weaving together the rich emotional fabric they bestow upon the child's journey.

The cherished presence of parents, siblings, mentors, or even dear friends during a child's formative voyage acts as steadfast anchors or inspiring catalysts for growth.

Whether it's a reassuring handheld tightly on that first day of school or an encouraging smile during a tough moment, these supportive figures play an invaluable role in shaping the child's confidence and curiosity. The stories shared, lessons imparted, and laughter enjoyed creating a nurturing environment where a child feels safe to explore their world, ask questions, and express themselves freely.

As the child grows, these early experiences become the foundation upon which they build their understanding of relationships, empathy, and resilience. The bonds formed through shared experiences and mutual support forge a sense of belonging and self-worth that carries them through life's challenges and triumphs. Each milestone, celebrated together, becomes a cherished chapter in the child's life story, reminding them of the love and encouragement that surrounds them.

In this way, family and friends are not just witnesses to a child's growth, but active participants in their journey, contributing threads to the vibrant tapestry of their life. Through the years, these connections deepen and develop, continuing to inspire and guide them as they step confidently into the future.

I vividly recall the enchanting day our daughter embarked on her kindergarten adventure. We carried her to the school, guiding her to the door of her classroom. Yet, in that precious moment, her blossoming independence took flight. With a brave spirit, she instructed us to remain outside, promising to venture in alone, to greet her teacher, and to discover her seat adorned with her name. As we stood together, tears glistening in our eyes, we clasped each other's hands, enveloped in a bittersweet embrace that marked this poignant transition for us both. We watched through the window as she stepped inside, her tiny figure radiating determination and excitement. Her backpack, as big as she was, bounced with each step, a symbol of the new adventures and knowledge she was about to embrace. As she turned to give us one last wave, her smile reassured us she was ready for this new chapter.

The classroom, filled with bright colors and the gentle hum of children's voices, became her new world—a place where she would learn, grow, and make her first friendships. Her teacher greeted her warmly, kneeling to her level, and we knew she was in kind, capable hands.

Returning home that day, the house felt a little quieter, a little emptier. We busied ourselves with chores, but our thoughts remained with her, wondering about her day, the stories she would bring back, and the unfamiliar words she would learn. We greeted her in return in the afternoon with open arms and eager questions, and she shared tales of her adventures with us, her eyes sparkling with excitement.

This experience marked not just her growth, but our own as well. We realized that while we were letting go, we were also holding on to the memories of her first steps into the world—a world that was bright and full of promise. And as she grew, we cherished each new milestone, knowing that each step she took was a step towards becoming her own person, with her own dreams and aspirations.

I once embarked on a journey to follow an eagle's nest and its enchanting hatchlings at a nearby college. They set up a live camera to capture the wonders of the nest. As the weeks unfurled, the hatchlings blossomed into their fledgling stage, frolicking at the very edge of their lofty perch. Soon, the fledglings took their inaugural flight, venturing into the great unknown, standing proudly on their own. It was a breathtaking, remarkable sight.

The eaglets, with their wings spread wide, seemed to embody the very essence of freedom and courage. Each flap of their wings was a testament to the nurturing care of their parents and the natural instincts that guided them. Observing their journey from tiny, fragile creatures to confident young birds ready to explore the world was a humbling experience. It reminded me of the intricate balance between protection and independence, a dance that all living beings partake in as they grow and mature.

The live camera allowed a community of viewers to connect with this remarkable story, sharing in the triumphs and challenges faced by the young eagles. It fostered a collective sense of wonder and appreciation for the natural world, as we all held our breath during those first tentative flights, hoping for their safe return. The eaglets' journey, much like that of my daughter on her first day of school, highlighted the universal journey of growth—a poignant reminder of the courage it takes to step into the unknown and the beauty found in each new beginning.

As the seasons changed, I continued to visit the site of the nest, occasionally glimpsing the young eagles soaring through the sky. Their presence was a comforting reminder of resilience and the enduring cycle of life. Nature, in all its wisdom, teaches us that while every journey starts with a single step or a hesitant flap of wings, it is the journey itself that shapes us, allowing us to soar beyond our wildest dreams.

As guardians, we behold the luminous **sparks of discovery** in our children—those precious instances when they unearth insights that reshape their perceptions of self and the universe. Be it a budding love for the arts or the profound contemplation of loss and transformation, these moments resonate with a deep and lasting impact. They serve as the gentle nudges that steer them toward their passions and purpose, helping to mold their character and identity. In the quietude of these revelations, we see the unfolding of their unique stories, each chapter rich with promise and potential.

We watch with pride as they **navigate the complexities of life**, each new understanding adding layers to their growing wisdom. Whether it's the awe of discovering a new book that opens their minds to uncharted worlds or the joy of mastering a musical instrument that becomes an outlet for their emotions, these experiences become the building blocks of their future.

Their exploration of the arts, sciences, or any captivating field reminds us of the boundless possibilities ahead. Their curiosity becomes a beacon, guiding them through the challenges and joys of life, and encouraging them to view each obstacle as an opportunity for growth.

In these moments of discovery, we see reflections of our own journeys. We remember the mentors and loved ones who supported us, and we strive to offer the same encouragement and guidance. We learn alongside them, sometimes reawakening our own sense of wonder and rekindling our passions.

These luminous sparks of discovery are not just pivotal for the children, but for us as well. They remind us of the beauty in learning, the importance of fostering creativity, and the joy of witnessing the unfolding of a vibrant life. Each revelation, each newfound interest, is a thread in the intricate tapestry of their lives, and we feel privileged to be part of this extraordinary journey.

The emergence of **societal norms, traditions, and cultural expectations** gently begins to sculpt the essence of our children's identities. Influences such as geography, faith, and socioeconomic factors lay the very groundwork of who we are as young souls and the paths we will tread.

The wondrous opportunities for exploration through play, where creativity flourishes and imagination take flight, form a cornerstone of childhood. Be it constructing grand castles in the sand or conjuring fantastical realms with naught but a humble cardboard box, these enchanting experiences nurture innovation and emotional development. Through the magic of play, children learn to navigate the intricate dance of social interactions, solve puzzles of life, and express their innermost selves in ways that transcend mere words. The simple act of playing becomes a powerful tool for growth, teaching children about collaboration, negotiation, and empathy. In these moments, they become architects of their own worlds, unbound by the constraints of reality, free to experiment and dream.

As they engage in play, children also encounter the first hints of responsibility and decision-making. Whether deciding on the rules of a game or choosing roles in a pretend scenario, they gain insights into leadership and compromise. These experiences, though small, lay the groundwork for future interactions, equipping them with skills that will serve them throughout their lives.

Parents and caregivers, observing from the sidelines, often find joy in witnessing the boundless enthusiasm and creativity that play inspires. It is a reminder of the pure, unfiltered joy that comes from exploration and discovery. Encouraging this type of play not only enhances a child's development but also strengthens the bonds between parent and child, as shared laughter and mutual understanding grow.

In the end, **play** is much more than a pastime; it is a vital component of childhood that shapes how children perceive the world and their place within it. It fosters resilience and adaptability, teaching them that even in the face of challenges, there is always room for growth and imagination. As they play, children not only learn about themselves but also about the diverse tapestry of humanity, preparing them to step into the world with confidence and curiosity.

In the gentle embrace of youth, the seeds of dreams and aspirations unfurl as children encounter a tapestry of new ideas, captivating tales, and inspiring role models. These nascent dreams, born from beloved storybook figures or real-life champions, ignite a flame of ambition and purpose. They become guiding stars, casting their luminous glow upon the pathways that children might traverse as they embark on the wondrous journey into adulthood. With each story read and each hero admired, children envision the possibilities that lie ahead. They see themselves as explorers, inventors, or artists who make the world more beautiful and moving. The encouragement of those around them—parents, teachers, and friends—who foster a belief in their potential and the courage to pursue their passions nurtured these dreams, still tender and malleable.

As they grow, children encounter challenges and triumphs that add depth and dimension to their dreams. They learn the value of perseverance and the importance of resilience, understanding that setbacks are not the end but steppingstones to success. Along the way, they gather wisdom and experience, shaping their aspirations into tangible goals.

The diversity of experiences and the multitude of voices that influence their path enriches the journey of self-discovery. Whether it's through the pages of a book, the words of a mentor, or the shared experiences with peers, each interaction adds a brushstroke to the developing canvas of their identity. In this vibrant landscape, they find the confidence to dream boldly and the determination to carve their own unique path.

These early dreams are more than just fantasies; they are the foundation upon which children build their future. They inspire a lifelong journey of exploration and growth, encouraging them to contribute positively to the world around them. As they step into adulthood, these dreams—rooted in the imaginative wonder of childhood—continue to guide them, lighting the way with hope and possibility.

As the tapestry of childhood unfurls, the emergence of **personal trials**—whether they be minor stumbles or formidable mountains—holds a vital place in the cultivation of resilience. These fleeting instances impart profound wisdom on perseverance, adaptability, and the power nestled within vulnerability. By triumphing over adversity, young souls come to understand that failure is not a final curtain but a steppingstone leading toward growth and the enchantment of self-discovery. Each challenge faced becomes a lesson in courage, teaching children that setbacks are simply opportunities in disguise. Through these experiences, they learn to trust in their abilities and find strength in their unique qualities. Whether it's overcoming a fear, solving a difficult problem, or navigating the complexities of friendships, each trial adds a layer to their understanding of themselves and the world around them.

In these moments, the support of family, friends, and mentors is invaluable. Their encouragement and belief in the child's potential help to foster a safe environment where taking risks and making mistakes are essential parts of learning. With love and guidance, children see every obstacle is surmountable, and every failure holds the seeds of future success.

As they grow, children build resilience on the bedrock of these personal trials, enabling them to face life's inevitable challenges with confidence and grace. Children learn that, although the path may be fraught with difficulties; This understanding empowers them to embrace their journey with an open heart and a courageous spirit, ready to explore the limitless possibilities that lie ahead.

In this way, the tapestry of childhood weaves together moments of joy, discovery, and challenge, creating a rich and vibrant narrative that shapes the individuals they will become. As they step into the world, equipped with the wisdom gleaned from their early experiences, they carry with them the resilience, empathy, and hope that will illuminate their path and inspire those around them.

In intertwining these elements, the tale of childhood unfolds as a splendid tapestry of arrivals—each a crucial thread in the grand narrative of personal evolution and identity. The chapter blossoms with the warmth of shared moments, the vivid hues of varied influences, and the tender reminder that every arrival, whether grand or modest, plays a part in the singular journey of becoming.

Each arrival gifts children with opportunities to discover themselves and the world around them. These experiences, marked by the firsts in their lives, are not just milestones but cherished memories that enrich their tapestry. The laughter shared in a sunlit park, the whispered secrets between newfound friends, and the comforting presence of loved ones during bedtime stories—all contribute to the intricate design of their growing identity.

As they journey through this vibrant landscape, children learn to weave their unique patterns of values, dreams, and aspirations. They understand the importance of kindness, the power of imagination, and the beauty of diversity. Each encounter, each lesson, becomes a golden thread, adding depth and texture to their unfolding narrative.

The influences of family, friends, educators, and the broader community play a pivotal role in shaping this tapestry. They offer guidance, encouragement, and wisdom, helping children navigate the complexities of life with empathy and resilience. This support fosters a sense of belonging, empowering young souls to explore their potential and embrace the unknown with courage.

In this beautiful tapestry of childhood, every moment is significant, no matter how small. It is a celebration of growth, a testament to the endless possibilities that await. As children continue to weave their stories, they carry with them the love and lessons of those who have journeyed alongside them, lighting the way toward a future filled with promise and wonder.

9

Letter to my 20-year-old Self

Dear Twenty-year-old Me:

Greetings, youthful dreamer! I sense you are brimming with grand aspirations and a sprinkle of trepidation about the journey ahead. Know this: you stand at the threshold of some of the most transformative years that life offers.

In this moment, love may feel like an enchanting riddle, abundant with hope and questions. Trust me, you will come to grasp its essence in ways you've yet to envision. One day, a soul will enter your life who truly perceives you—the radiant, the imperfect, the entirety of your being—and loves you for all that you are. When that magic occurs, treasure it. Crafting a shared life demands effort, patience, and a generous helping of laughter, yet it will blossom into one of the most fulfilling quests you'll undertake.

As for children? They will impart lessons in love, resilience, and joy beyond your wildest dreams. They'll turn your universe upside down, but in the most wondrous manner. Embrace the delightful chaos, even on days when it feels like you're merely trying to keep pace. Remember, being present for them doesn't require perfection; it's about showing up, listening, and loving them fiercely.

Regarding your career and aspirations—never lose sight of them. These are the years to take bold leaps and pursue what ignites your passion. There will be hurdles, detours, and moments where surrender seems tempting. Resist that urge. Each step, even the missteps, will carve the path to your true self.

Last, remember to nurture yourself. It's all too easy to pour every ounce of energy into others, but don't forget to tend to your own well-being. The stronger and healthier you become, the more you'll have to share with those you cherish.

Keep your heart open, your spirit resilient, and your gaze fixed on the horizon. Extraordinary adventures await you.

With all my love,

Your Older, Wiser Self

P.S. Don't underestimate the power of small moments. Quiet, everyday experiences reveal some of the most profound joys and insights. Whether it's a walk in the park, a heartfelt conversation with a friend, or a solitary evening spent with an enjoyable book, these moments are the threads that weave the tapestry of your life.

Cherish your friendships, old and new. They are the anchors that will keep you grounded and the wings that will help you soar. Nurture these connections with sincerity and kindness, for they will be your greatest support and joy in times of both celebration and challenge.

And always, always remember to dream. Dream without limits and let your imagination take flight. It's through dreaming that you'll discover fresh paths and possibilities, and it's through action that you'll bring them to life.

So, dear one, keep dreaming, keep striving, and keep believing in the beautiful future that lies ahead. You are capable of more than you can imagine, and the world is ready for all the light you offer.

10

Midlife – The Long Station Stop

Midlife often resembles a bustling airport terminal, doesn't it? The people, roles, and certainties you've cherished seem to ascend into the heavens, leaving behind a swirl of nostalgia, heartache, and deep introspection. This chapter of life becomes adorned with metaphorical "departures," those poignant moments when the anchors of our existence transform or drift away altogether. Yet, amidst the flurry of change and the echoes of footsteps fading into the distance, there is also a palpable sense of anticipation. Just as travelers await their flights, so, too, do we find ourselves poised at the gate of new opportunities and experiences. It's a time to embrace the unknown with courage and curiosity, to welcome the "arrivals" that promise to enrich our lives in unexpected ways.

In this phase, we might discover new passions that ignite our spirits or forge connections with individuals who bring fresh perspectives and companionship. It's a reminder that life is not a fixed itinerary, but a journey filled with detours and discoveries. Each farewell, though tinged with sadness, clears the path for new beginnings that can lead to profound personal growth and fulfillment.

As we navigate this terminal of life, we learn to carry the memories of what was with gratitude, while keeping our hearts open to the wonders that lie ahead. This delicate balance of letting go and embracing the new defines the essence of midlife, a transformative period that invites us to soar to new heights, grounded in the past's wisdom.

The departure of parents can evoke the sensation of a mighty tree, its roots stripped away, leaving behind a void of stability and heritage. As you grow apart from cherished souls—be it a sibling or a dear friend—you may find yourself adrift on divergent currents in an ocean once traversed in unison. Career transitions, whether embraced or imposed, can shake the very foundations of your sense of purpose and identity. These partings are inescapably bittersweet; they herald closures while simultaneously beckoning the promise of personal growth. Yet, it's in these very moments of transition that we often uncover the depth of our resilience and adaptability. Just as a tree might spread new roots to find nourishment elsewhere, so, too, do we learn to establish new connections and support systems. Losing familiar roles and relationships can compel us to look within, rediscovering facets of ourselves that the routines and responsibilities of the past had overshadowed.

This phase of life invites us to redefine what truly matters, to embrace the opportunity to craft a narrative that reflects our growing values and aspirations. As we navigate these waters, we might find that the currents carry us to unexpected destinations, places where we can grow in ways we never imagined. Although difficult, this process offers the chance to improve and transform.

Midlife is not just a period of loss, but also a canvas for creation. Each goodbye offers the gift of space for new hellos, and every end marks the beginning of a new chapter filled with the promise of discovery and joy. It's about learning to dance with the rhythm of change, finding beauty in the ebb and flow of life's seasons, and cherishing the wisdom and strength that comes from embracing both departures and arrivals with an open heart.

Yet, amidst these bittersweet farewells, a symphony of "arrivals" awaits, ready to grace the runway of midlife with newfound vibrance. Grandchildren radiate boundless joy, offering the exquisite chance to witness the world anew through the sparkling eyes of a younger generation. Embarking on new hobbies can unveil a rejuvenating journey, infusing fresh purpose into days that may have felt ensnared in stillness. Perhaps most profoundly, midlife often heralds a wisdom cultivated from cherished reflections—a deeper understanding of oneself, the strength within, and the exquisite beauty of life's fleeting moments.

Though departures may leave a tender ache, these arrivals remind us that growth, connection, and meaning are steadfast companions—ever eager to embrace us in our current state. How does this resonate within your heart? Would you care to delve deeper into any aspect?

Threads of both melancholy and exuberance indeed weave the tapestry of midlife. As you ponder these arrivals, consider the remarkable opportunity to redefine the landscape of your life. For instance, grandchildren bring joy and invite you to step back into a world of wonder and curiosity—a world where even the simplest moments fill with magic and discovery.

These new hobbies and pursuits invite us to become students once again, reminding us that learning never truly ends. Whether it's painting, gardening, or exploring the great outdoors, these activities can rekindle a zest for life that routine has dimmed. They serve as a testament to the fact that creativity and passion can flourish at any age.

We cannot overstate the value of the wisdom that emerges during this time. It allows for a deeper appreciation of life's nuances and the ability to find peace amidst chaos. This wisdom is a gentle guide, helping to navigate the complexities of relationships, personal growth, and the inevitable changes that accompany this stage of life.

Reflecting on these elements can inspire a profound sense of gratitude and fulfillment. Embrace this phase as a dance with life itself—a dance where every step, whether forward or backward, contributes to the rich, growing story of who you are. As you continue this journey, remember that each arrival is not just a continuation but a new beginning, filled with endless possibilities and the potential for joy.

The Departures:

Loss of Parents: This moment transcends a mere farewell to cherished ones; it signifies a profound transformation in the very essence of your identity. Parents often embody the roots of our existence—anchoring us to heritage, imparting wisdom, and offering stability. Their departure evokes not only sorrow but also the sensation of entering an unexplored chapter of life, wherein you ascend to the role of the "older generation." It invites contemplation on mortality and the legacies we leave behind, often inspiring a deeper introspection on the life you wish to cultivate as you journey onward.

It is a time when you may reflect on the values and traditions you wish to preserve and pass down, as well as the new ones you hope to create. This transition challenges you to guide future generations, sharing wisdom and building fresh memories.

As you navigate this uncharted territory, you may feel a renewed sense of purpose, driven by the desire to be a source of strength and love for those around you. The realization that you are now a part of the older generation can be both daunting and empowering, prompting you to consider how you can positively influence the lives of others and continue to grow personally.

In this new role, there is an opportunity to redefine what it means to be a mentor, a leader, and a cherished family member. It is a call to engage with life fully, to share stories and experiences, and to be a beacon of hope and encouragement. As you forge ahead, remember that each moment, whether filled with joy or challenge, contributes to the rich tapestry of your life and the legacy you will leave behind. Embrace this chapter with an open heart, knowing that your journey is far from over and that endless possibilities await on the horizon.

Growing Apart from Loved Ones: This transformation can unfold as subtly and gradually as the slow waltz of tectonic plates beneath the earth's crust. It may reveal itself in a sibling whose path has diverged, in a friendship that has dimmed under the burdens of time and distance, or even in the tender strains of a relationship with an adult child. Such departures, often shrouded in invisibility, resonate profoundly, leaving behind a bittersweet ache and a rich tapestry of unanswered questions about the evolution of our connections. They invite us to embrace the beauty of impermanence and to find comfort in cherishing the echoes of what once was.

Amidst these changes, we learn to appreciate the transient nature of relationships and the enduring impact they have on our lives. Separation reminds us of the importance of resilience and adaptability as we seek new ways to nurture our connections and keep the spirit of love and understanding alive.

As we navigate these shifts, it's essential to focus on the memories and lessons shared, allowing them to guide us as we forge fresh paths. The bonds we've formed, though altered, continue to shape us, offering wisdom and strength as we journey forward. In embracing the fluidity of life, we open ourselves to the possibility of rekindling old ties or discovering new ones that resonate with our present selves.

Ultimately, these departures encourage us to live authentically and to cherish the moments we share with those we love. They remind us that while some paths may diverge, the essence of our connections remains, woven into the fabric of our being, ready to support us as we embrace the unknown with an open heart. In this dance of life, every step—whether towards or away from familiar faces—adds to the richness of our story, a testament to the enduring power of love and human connection.

Career Shifts: In the twilight of one's career, be it through retirement, downsizing, or embracing an alternative path, midlife transitions unveil a dual enchantment: the quest to redefine success and rekindle purpose. These transformations gently peel away the external symbols of accomplishment, urging a moment of introspection: *Who am I when I'm not defined by my vocation?* This challenging question can be a starting point for learning more about yourself and changing your life. This question urges us to look within and explore passions and interests.

In this newfound freedom, many find the opportunity to pursue dreams that were once distant whispers. Whether it's volunteering for a cause close to the heart, authoring that novel that has been waiting to be penned, or simply spending more time in nature, these pursuits can lead to a profound sense of fulfillment and joy.

The shedding of career-related identities also invites us to reassess our values and what truly brings meaning to our lives. It is a chance to cultivate skills and relationships that nurture the soul, enriching our days with a sense of purpose that transcends professional achievements.

This phase focuses not on what we left behind, but on what lies ahead—recent adventures, continued growth, and the joy of living life on our own terms. Embrace this chapter with an open mind and heart, ready to explore the myriad possibilities that await.

The Arrivals:

Grandchildren and Family Expansion: Grandchildren grace the holiday table not merely with fresh faces, but with an abundance of joy, renewal, and the delightful opportunity to nurture without the weight of parenting's duties. Embracing this cherished role awakens a singular bond, a gentle reminder of love's eternal cycle and the wondrous rhythms of life. Their laughter fills the room, weaving a melody that echoes the innocence and wonder of youth. Simple pleasures light up their eyes, reminding you of the magic in everyday moments. This connection invites you to step into their world, where imagination reigns supreme and each day is an adventure.

These gatherings become a tapestry of shared stories and traditions, infused with the vibrancy of new beginnings. You revisit old tales with fresh enthusiasm, eager to pass down wisdom wrapped in warmth and affection. The presence of grandchildren allows you to relive cherished memories while creating new ones, painting a picture of a family that spans generations.

In this role, you have the privilege of being both a storyteller and a listener, an encouraging guide, and a playful companion. The wisdom of your years combines with the innocence of theirs, creating a unique and beautiful harmony. It's a relationship built on love, patience, and understanding, where each moment shared is a gift that enriches your soul.

Through their eyes, you rediscover the world anew, finding joy in the simple and the ordinary. You remember what truly matters—the connections binding us and the loving legacy we leave. Embrace these moments, for they offer not only the chance to nurture young hearts but also to nurture your own, filling your days with purpose and your heart with boundless joy.

New Hobbies and Passions: As certain roles gracefully wane, new ones blossom forth. Perhaps you embrace the art of painting, master the melodies of an instrument, or uncover hidden hiking trails that beckon your spirit. These pursuits transcend mere pastimes—they serve as vital lifelines, bestowing not only delightful distraction but also infusing your life with purpose, rekindling a spark of curiosity, and wrapping you in the warm embrace of accomplishment.

As you immerse yourself in these new endeavors, you find they offer more than just moments of joy; they become pathways to self-expression and avenues for personal growth. Each brushstroke on a canvas, each note played, and each step taken along a forest path becomes a testament to your journey of discovery. These activities provide a sense of fulfillment and a reminder that life is an ever-developing adventure, filled with opportunities to learn and grow.

In exploring these passions, you may connect with like-minded individuals, forming communities that enrich your experience and provide support and encouragement. These connections foster a sense of belonging and remind you that you are not alone on this journey. Together, you share stories, celebrate achievements, and inspire each other to reach new heights.

Engaging in new hobbies also invites you to see the world through fresh eyes, reigniting a sense of wonder and appreciation for the beauty that surrounds you. Whether you're capturing a breathtaking sunset with your camera or learning the intricate steps of a dance, these activities allow you to savor the present moment and find joy in the simple pleasures of life.

As you continue to explore these new horizons, remember that each step forward is a celebration of your resilience, adaptability, and zest for life. Embrace the challenges and triumphs, knowing that they are all part of the rich tapestry of your personal narrative. Guide your heart with curiosity and courage; let these pursuits illuminate the path ahead with endless possibilities and the promise of fulfillment.

Wisdom Through Reflection: Midlife gives the treasure of perspective. By this juncture, you have braved enough tempests to discern which truly matter and which fade into whispers. Wisdom does not arrive with a grand proclamation but softly revealing the ephemeral beauty, preciousness, and intricate ties that bind all things. It heralds the emergence of gratitude, the grace of forgiveness, and a deeper wellspring of love. This newfound clarity allows you to navigate life's complexities with a gentler, more compassionate outlook. It's a time when you recognize the importance of savoring each moment, understanding that life's true richness lies in the simple pleasures and the connections we nurture.

As you stand at this crossroads, you may reflect on past experiences, not with regret, but with appreciation for the lessons they imparted. Each challenge faced has contributed to the tapestry of your life, adding depth and texture to your story. This perspective encourages you to embrace change with an open heart, ready to welcome new opportunities and experiences.

In this phase, the wisdom gained becomes a guiding light, illuminating your path forward. It inspires you to prioritize what truly resonates with your soul and to let go of what no longer serves your growth. You realize true fulfillment comes not from external achievements, but from rich relationships and the joy of presence in each moment.

This wisdom empowers you to live authentically and intentionally, creating a life that reflects your deepest values and aspirations. You learn to dance gracefully with the rhythm of life, appreciating both its highs and lows, and finding beauty in every step along the way. Embrace this treasure of perspective, for it is a gift that will continue to enrich your journey, offering peace, joy, and a profound sense of connection to the world around you.

<u>Between the Departures and Arrivals</u>:

Life now invites you to dwell within the delicate interludes—the sorrow that shadows loss and the gratitude that blooms from rebirth. It is a dance of equilibrium: honoring what once was, treasuring the present, and inviting the future. Within this sacred space lies the wisdom of resilience, adaptability, and the journey of self-discovery.

This period is a call to be gentle with yourself, to acknowledge the complexities of your emotions, and to find strength in vulnerability. As you navigate these transitions, you may find solace in the quiet moments of reflection, where you can connect with your innermost thoughts and feelings.

Embracing this balance requires patience and self-compassion. It means allowing yourself the time to grieve the endings while also celebrating the new beginnings. It's about recognizing that each experience, whether joyful or challenging, contributes to your growth and enriches your understanding of life.

In these interludes, you can cultivate a deeper connection with yourself and the world around you. It's a time to explore what truly matters to you, to seek experiences that align with your values, and to nurture relationships that bring meaning and joy. As you do so, you create a life that is both authentic and fulfilling, guided by the wisdom that arises from embracing life's ebb and flow.

Ultimately, this journey is about finding peace in the present moment, trusting that each step forward—no matter how small—brings you closer to a life filled with purpose, joy, and endless possibilities. Embrace this dance of equilibrium with an open heart, knowing that every experience is a valuable thread in the rich tapestry of your life.

11

Letter to my 50-year-old Self

Dearest 50-Year-Old Me,

What a wondrous milestone you've reached! I hope this message finds you basking in a life that feels both meaningful and authentic. Take a moment to reflect on the majestic journey that has brought you here.

By now, you've discovered that life often dances to its own rhythm, diverging from the plans you once crafted in your youth—and that is perfectly all right. It is within those unexpected twists that the true magic unfolds. I hope you've embraced the art of stumbling, growing, and finding joy amidst the beautifully imperfect.

If you haven't yet, carve out time for the passions that ignite your spirit, whether they are in creation, connection, or exploration. Let not the cacophony of the world drown out your inner wisdom—it always knows the path forward. And should you find yourself feeling overwhelmed, remember to pause and breathe; you possess strength and capability beyond your imagination.

Continue to chase your dreams, yet don't forget to savor the little wonders—a shared laugh with a friend, the gentle warmth of sunlight upon your skin, or the serene stillness of a quiet morning. These fleeting moments weave the rich tapestry of a life well-lived.

Cherish the relationships that have stood the test of time and never underestimate the power of kindness and compassion—they are the threads that bind us all together. As you navigate the complexities of adulthood, remember that it's okay to seek help and lean on those who care for you. You are never alone on this journey.

I hope you continue to cultivate gratitude, for it is a lens through which life becomes brighter and more fulfilling. Embrace change as an old friend, for it is the only constant, and with it comes growth and renewal. Trust in your resilience and the lessons learned from both triumphs and trials.

May you find the courage to pursue what sets your soul on fire, even if it means taking the road less traveled. The world is vast and full of wonders, waiting for you to explore its many facets. Keep your heart open to new experiences and let curiosity guide you.

Remember to be gentle with yourself. Life is not a race, but a journey to be savored, one step at a time. With each passing year, you are crafting a legacy uniquely your own—a legacy of love, wisdom, and adventure.

Until we meet again, continue to shine brightly, and live authentically. The future is yours to create, and I know it will be extraordinary.

With endless hope and admiration,

Your 74-Year-Old Self

12

Later Years – A Time of Perspective

In the twilight years of existence, the frenetic pace of youth gracefully mellows into a serene cadence. This sacred chapter invites reflection, offering wisdom sculpted by the seasons of joy, sorrow, and metamorphosis. It is a moment where the comings and goings of midlife coalesce into a profound comprehension of life's gentle ebb and flow. The twilight becomes a canvas for introspection, where the vivid colors of past experiences merge into a soft, harmonious palette. Here, time feels less like a relentless pursuit and more like a gentle companion, guiding you through a landscape of memories and dreams. It is a time for gentle contemplation, where the heart finds solace in the understanding that each moment, whether joyous or challenging, has contributed to the rich tapestry of your life.

As you navigate this phase, there is an opportunity to embrace the beauty of simplicity. You may cherish the quiet moments—those small, insignificant instants that, in hindsight, hold profound significance. A walk in the garden, the laughter of a grandchild, the warmth of a sunset—all become treasures that illuminate the path ahead.

This period encourages a deepened connection with oneself and others, fostering relationships that are rooted in authenticity and compassion. It is a time to share stories, to impart wisdom, and to learn anew from the growing world around you. The twilight years are not just a conclusion but a celebration—a tribute to a life well-lived and a testament to the enduring spirit that carries forward with grace and dignity.

The Departures

Reaching this pivotal stage often invites one to grapple with the undeniable truth that life unfolds as a tapestry woven with goodbyes. The departure of cherished souls—parents, siblings, and dear friends—leaves a void that resonates deeply within the heart. The gradual ebbing of physical vigor also becomes apparent, as our bodies transform into more delicate allies. Familiar roles, such as those of a devoted professional or primary caregiver, gracefully recede into the shadows. While these farewells carry a weight of sorrow, they also emerge as profound mentors, gently reminding us of life's fleeting nature and urging us to treasure each precious moment.

Yet, within this tapestry of departures lies an intricate beauty. Each goodbye, though tinged with sadness, is a testament to the connections and experiences that have enriched your journey. Gratitude for shared time, lessons learned, and love exchanged weaves these moments of parting. They serve as gentle reminders to embrace the present and cherish the relationships that remain.

Amidst these farewells, there is also a quiet strength that emerges. It is the resilience born from understanding that life is a series of cycles, each bringing its own gifts and challenges. This perspective allows you to face change with grace, knowing that every ending opens the door to new beginnings. The twilight years, therefore, become not just a time of reflection, but also one of renewal, where the heart is open to the possibilities that still lie ahead.

In this space, you find an opportunity to redefine your identity, no longer constrained by societal roles or expectations. It is a time to explore passions long set aside, to seek fresh adventures, and to cultivate a sense of joy in simply being. The departures may mark the closing of certain chapters, but they also pave the way for fresh narratives rich with potential and discovery.

This stage of life, with all its departures and arrivals, is a dance of continuity and change. It invites you to hold on to the memories that nourish your spirit, while courageously stepping into the unknown with an open heart. Here, you find peace knowing that each moment, each goodbye, is a vital part of the story that is uniquely yours.

The Arrivals

Yet, amidst the farewells, new beginnings spring forth, bestowing renewed purpose and joy. The arrival of grandchildren breathes life into the soul with an expansive and unencumbered love—a chance to witness the unfolding of your legacy. There are also the newfound passions you can finally embrace: diving into stacks of books, nurturing a vibrant garden, or losing yourself in the world of art. Most profoundly, there's serenity—a deep contentment that blossoms from relinquishing the need to rush, to conquer, or to prove oneself. This is the season of simplicity and heartfelt gratitude.

It is a time when the heart swells with appreciation for the simple pleasures that fill each day. We savor these moments—the gentle rustle of leaves in the breeze or the comforting aroma of a homemade meal—with an intensity that only comes from understanding their fleeting nature. The arrivals in this stage of life bring with them a sense of completion and fulfillment, as if every step of the journey has led to this harmonious balance between past and present.

In this embrace of the present, you reconnect with the world in ways previously unimagined. Long-lost friendships might rekindle, offering fresh perspectives and shared laughter that enrich the soul. Opportunities to mentor and inspire younger generations become avenues for sharing the wisdom accumulated over the years, creating bonds that bridge the ages.

The arrivals also invite you to look inward, to explore the depths of your own being with curiosity and compassion. It is a chance to understand yourself more fully, to acknowledge and accept all facets of your life's story. This self-discovery is not just introspective but also liberating, freeing you from past burdens and allowing you to step into the future with renewed confidence.

Thus, the twilight years become a vibrant dance of farewells and welcomes, a celebration of all that has been and all that is yet to come. This is a time for both reflection and action, where each goodbye promises a new hello, and each ending opens a gateway to fresh beginnings.

The Lens of Perspective

With the passage of time, age bestows a wisdom that youth frequently overlook. It reshapes our perspective, illuminating what is genuinely important. Success shifts from a collection of accolades to the richness of our connections, the kindness we extend, and the cherished memories we weave. Challenges that once loomed large now appear diminutive against the vast canvas of a life richly experienced. Regret gently fades, giving way to a serene acceptance of both stumbles and victories as vibrant threads in the grand tapestry of existence.

In this light, age becomes not a burden, but a gift—a reminder to savor each moment with intention and gratitude. A more measured pace replaces the urgency of youth and its relentless pursuit of what's next; every sunrise brings wonder, and every sunset offers a chance to reflect on the day's beauty.

In these years, you find yourself more attuned to the world around you. Nature's cycles mirror the rhythms of your own life, offering solace and inspiration. The laughter of children, the rustle of leaves, and the gentle murmur of a stream become melodies that resonate deeply, reminding you of the interconnectedness of all things.

This shift in perspective also encourages a deeper sense of empathy and understanding. Having traversed the peaks and valleys of life, you possess a reservoir of compassion that enables you to connect with others on a profound level. You listen more intently, speak with sincerity, and hold space for those you love, fostering relationships that are both nurturing and fulfilling.

Ultimately, the wisdom of age allows you to embrace life's impermanence with an open heart. You begin to see the beauty in change and the potential in every new day. This is a time to celebrate the journey, to honor the past, and to welcome the future with hope and curiosity. In this stage, what defines you is not your achievements, but how you have lived and loved.

The Role of Memory

In the twilight of life, memory assumes a hallowed mantle, transforming into a treasure trove of tales, wisdom, and cherished moments awaiting rediscovery. Though the mind may occasionally play tricks—memories can blur and wane—the ones that endure often radiate with a luminous poignancy. Even the ephemeral echoes of laughter, love, and significant milestones serve as steadfast anchors, tethering you to a profound sense of identity and connection.

Memories become a tapestry woven from the threads of your experiences, each one a vibrant hue in the mosaic of your life. They are the stories you revisit with a gentle smile; the lessons learned that guide your steps, and the warmth of past embraces that linger in your heart.

In this sacred dance with memory, there is a celebration of all that has been—a tribute to the journey that has shaped you. You find solace in recalling the moments of triumph and the muted resilience that carried you through challenges. The faces of loved ones, whether near or long departed, appear as vivid reminders of the love and support that have surrounded you throughout the years.

These recollections also offer a unique lens through which to view the present. They remind you of the impermanence of life, encouraging an embrace of each day with gratitude and attentiveness. In this way, memory is not just a reflection of what was, but a bridge to the now, enriching your appreciation for the life you continue to live.

As you nurture these memories, you also become a storyteller, sharing your journey with those who follow in your footsteps. Through your tales, you impart wisdom and understanding, leaving a legacy that transcends time. This sharing not only preserves your experiences but also strengthens the bonds between generations, ensuring that the essence of your life endures and inspires.

In the twilight years, memory becomes a source of strength and serenity—a reminder that the beauty of life lies not just in its grand events, but in the small, cherished moments that weave the fabric of your story.

Legacy

The notion of legacy emerges as a guiding star. It transcends mere material inheritance, delving into the ethereal imprint one leaves upon the tapestry of existence. It encompasses the values shared, the lives enriched, and the tales that flourish through children, grandchildren, and all whom you've inspired. Legacy is akin to sowing seeds for trees under whose canopy you may never dwell—yet finding profound joy in that very truth.

Legacy is the culmination of a life lived with intention and purpose, a testament to the impact you've made on the world and the people within it. It is the gentle handprint on the hearts of those who continue to carry your spirit forward; the wisdom passed down through generations, and the kindness that echoes long after you are gone.

In this sense, legacy becomes a living, breathing entity—an ongoing narrative that develops with each person who carries it. It is the love that inspires others to dream, to act with compassion, and to find the courage to pursue their own paths. You weave your legacy into the fabric of their lives, shaping their stories as those before you shaped yours.

Embracing the notion of legacy invites a sense of fulfillment, knowing that your life has been a conduit for positive change and inspiration. It encourages you to live with authenticity, guided by the values and principles you hold dear. Every action, no matter how small, becomes a part of this enduring legacy, illustrating the profound truth that even the simplest gestures can create ripples of lasting impact.

As you reflect on the legacy you wish to leave, it is also a call to nurture relationships, to foster understanding, and to celebrate the connections that define our shared humanity. This mindful approach to living ensures that your legacy is not just a memory, but a vibrant force that continues to uplift and empower.

Legacy is a gift—a way of ensuring that the essence of who you are and what you believe in endures, touching lives in ways you could never have imagined. It is a reminder that, in the grand tapestry of existence, your story is an integral thread, contributing to the beauty and richness of the whole.

The Joy in Quiet Moments

At last, the twilight years unveil a profound reverence for the beauty found in stillness. The gentle embrace of a warm cup of tea as golden sunlight dances through a window. Birds flitting gracefully through the garden is a tranquil delight. The simple joy of clasping a loved one's hand, where no words are necessary. These fleeting moments, once brushed aside, now resonate with a depth of meaning that feels almost divine.

In this chapter of existence, the farewells teach the art of letting go. The new beginnings inspire you to keep your heart wide open. Through the lens of experience, life is not about clinging to what once was, but about embracing the present—with grace, wisdom, and heartfelt gratitude.

Each quiet moment becomes a cherished jewel in the tapestry of your life, reflecting the light of countless memories and the promise of what lies ahead. It's in these serene pauses that you discover a deeper connection to the world around you, as if nature itself is whispering its secrets into your soul. The rhythm of your days slows to a gentle cadence, allowing you to savor the richness of each experience fully.

In this peaceful state, creativity often finds a new home. Perhaps you take up painting, writing, or music—expressions that allow your inner world to unfold in vibrant colors and melodies. These creative endeavors are not merely hobbies; they are expressions of the soul, a way to capture the essence of emotions that words alone cannot convey.

These twilight years provide a platform for gratitude to flourish. With each sunrise, you greet the day with a heart full of appreciation for the simple pleasures that life offers. The laughter of family, the scent of blooming flowers, or the soothing sound of rain on the roof—each becomes an opportunity to reflect on the abundance that surrounds you.

The joy in quiet moments also invites a profound sense of contentment. As external achievements fade in importance, you find fulfillment in the richness of your inner life. This contentment is a gentle reminder that true happiness arises not from what you possess or accomplish, but from how deeply you engage with the world and those you love.

As you journey through the twilight years, you come to understand that the essence of life lies not in the grand events but in the quiet, unassuming moments that weave together your days. These are the moments that, in their simplicity, reveal the true beauty and meaning of a life well-lived.

13

Letter to my Future Self

Dear Future Me,

Greetings from the echoes of the past! By now, you've traversed a tapestry of experiences—victories, trials, and all the moments that lie between. I trust you've welcomed the wisdom each journey bestowed and discovered tranquility in the essence of who you are.

Pause for a heartbeat and reflect: Are you still pursuing the wonders that ignite your curiosity? Do you still find joy in laughter as you once did? I hope the answer sings a vibrant "yes." I hope you've cultivated your passions and cherished the bonds that hold the deepest significance.

Along your path, you've likely released many burdens—fears, resentments, perhaps even dreams that no longer resonate. This is a beautiful evolution. I hope you've embraced the dawn of new beginnings, even when they seemed daunting.

Lastly, thank you for honoring the vows I made to myself. Thank you for your resilience, for blossoming with grace, and for keeping your gaze fixed on what truly counts. Here's to the adventures that lie ahead—you are more than capable.

May you continue to savor the simple pleasures and embrace the beauty of life's small moments. Remember, it's never too late to learn, to grow, or to start anew. Keep your heart open to love in all its forms and let kindness guide your actions.

As you stand on the cusp of new horizons, remember to be gentle with yourself. Celebrate your achievements, both big and small, and forgive yourself for the times you stumbled. Life is an ever-evolving journey, and your story is one of resilience and grace.

With Love and Grace,

Your Present-Day Self

14

Beyond the Final Departure

Death stands as an inevitable passage, both feared and revered, yet it weaves a thread of unity among humanity in its shared enigma. The question of what lies beyond this final farewell remains one of life's greatest mysteries, with our approaches reflecting our deepest philosophies and beliefs.

For some, as espoused in Buddhism, death transforms into a transition—a gateway to rebirth within the endless cycle of samsara. The Tibetan Book of the Dead serves as a guiding light for traversing the Bardo, the liminal space between death and rebirth, reminding us of the fleeting nature of existence and the quest for enlightenment.

Conversely, the Christian tradition often perceives death as a climactic moment of judgment, where the faithful ascend to eternal life in heaven or face separation from the divine. The promise of resurrection imbues death with hope, reshaping it into a passage of ultimate reunion and redemption.

Indigenous traditions frequently celebrate the interconnectedness of life and death. Many Native American beliefs depict the spirit merging back with nature, its essence living on in the wind, the trees, or the stars. Here, death is not an end, but a return to the Great Spirit.

Hinduism offers yet another captivating viewpoint, wherein atman (the soul) departs the body to unite with Brahman, the universal spirit, or is reborn based on one's karma. This cyclical understanding resonates with the eternal rhythm of life, death, and rebirth.

Even science contributes a humbling sense of continuity: our bodies become part of the earth; our atoms are dispersed back into the cosmos. Carl Sagan poignantly points out that we are made of "star stuff."

What lingers behind is profound in its simplicity. It's the love we shared, the memories we crafted, and the impact we etched upon the lives of others. These intangibles form the legacy that bridges the physical and the metaphysical.

As for what lies beyond—it's best left shrouded in mystery. The unknown invites reflection, wonder, and faith. As poet Mary Oliver beautifully expressed, "When it's over, I want to say all my life / I was a bride married to amazement."

In the embrace of such diverse perspectives, we find a tapestry of understanding that enriches our collective narrative about death and the afterlife. Each belief system offers unique insights, yet they all converge on the notion of continuity, transformation, and the enduring essence of the human spirit.

In the quiet moments of contemplation, we might ponder our own beliefs and how they shape our approach to life and death. Whether we see death as a beginning, an end, or a transition, it serves as a poignant reminder to live fully and meaningfully. The stories we tell, the love we give, and the experiences we gather become the threads that weave the fabric of our existence, transcending the boundaries of time.

In the end, the greatest journey lies not in seeking definitive answers but in embracing the mystery with open hearts and minds. It is in this acceptance that we may find peace, joy, and a deeper connection to all that is—and all that may yet be.

Philosophical Views on Death:

Philosophers from myriad cultures and epochs have wrestled with the profound mystery of death, illuminating its essence and importance through a tapestry of diverse perspectives. Here unfolds a reflective exploration of some of the most influential thoughts on this eternal enigma:

1. **Stoicism**: Luminaries like Marcus Aurelius and Seneca regarded death as an intrinsic facet of existence. They urged us to embrace this inevitability with serenity, for it lies beyond our dominion. Instead, they championed a life of virtue in the present as the essence of true fulfillment.

2. **Existentialism**: Visionaries such as Jean-Paul Sartre and Martin Heidegger illuminated the awareness of death as pivotal to grasping the essence of life. For Sartre, the relentless approach of death magnifies the imperative to forge meaning in a cosmos stripped of inherent purpose.

Conversely, Heidegger posited that confronting our mortality is the gateway to living authentically.

3. **Epicureanism**: Epicurus proclaimed that death should be met with indifference, famously asserting, "When we exist, death does not exist. His teachings urged the pursuit of a serene existence, liberated from needless fears.

4. **Kantian Ethics**: Immanuel Kant contemplated the moral dimensions of mortality. He believed that the fleeting nature of life compels us to act with integrity and adhere to the moral law. Death, in his view, imparts urgency to our moral obligations, urging us to carve a meaningful existence.

5. **Eastern Philosophy**: In traditions like Taoism and Confucianism, death is often viewed as a harmonious continuation of the cosmic cycle. Taoist thought, for instance, sees death as a return to the Tao, the ultimate essence of all being, while Confucianism emphasizes living with moral integrity to leave a legacy.

6. **The Absurd (Albert Camus)**: Camus articulated the tension between our quest for meaning and the universe's silence, coining it "the absurd." Rather than succumbing to despair, he encouraged a spirited embrace of life, even in the face of its inevitable end.

7. **Transhumanist Views**: Contemporary perspectives, such as trans-humanism, regard death as a challenge to be overcome. Advocates explore avenues for extending life or achieving immortality through technological advancements, questioning the traditional acceptance of mortality.

8. **The Mystery of Being (Simone de Beauvoir)**: De Beauvoir contemplated death's profound influence on human freedom. She perceived death not as the negation of existence but as a moment that stresses the preciousness of life, urging us to live with authenticity and purpose.

These diverse viewpoints weave together a rich tapestry of thought, inviting us to reflect not only on death but also on how we might choose to live in its ever-present shadow.

15

What Happens When Aging

What Happens When Aging

Six pills in the morning, another five at night.
You would think I was dying, and you might be right!
Day after day, life gets harder to bear.
I'm losing my memory and also my hair.
It's up at 5:30, come rain or come shine.
Some days I feel like I'm losing my mind.
But deep in my heart, there's a flicker of light,
A stubborn resolve that continues to fight.
Though weary and worn, I'm still here to say,
Each sunrise whispers, "You've made it today."
The road may be rugged, the climb steep and tall,

But even when stumbling, I'm refusing to fall.
For life, though it's fragile, still holds its own charm,
In laughter, in moments, in love's embracing arm.
So, I'll take these pills and face every test,
With hope in my soul and strength in my chest.
For while the days may feel heavy with strife,
I'll savor the beauty in this precious life.
The Rev. Dr. Charles E. Cravey, March 2025

Epilogue

I began this journey by illuminating the significance of arrivals and departures that weave through the tapestry of our lives. You now possess a treasure trove of wisdom to forge your own choices concerning life, death, and all that lies in between, for it is in those fleeting years—the dash—that we truly dwell.

As you gaze into the horizon of your future, pause, and reflect on what holds the deepest meaning for you. Avoid drifting aimlessly through the unfolding days, lulled into the belief that all will align in time. Life has a whimsical way of presenting unexpected challenges. Embrace each dawn with intention, cherishing the moments to their fullest. Take a respite; embark on a journey; halt the relentless march of time whenever you can. As I shared about my dear friend in the hospital at the beginning of this narrative, there may come a time when the world must cater to your every need, or when your thoughts drift away from the vessel of your body.

Remember to nurture the connections that matter most, for they are the anchors that hold us steady in the turbulent seas of life. Cherish your loved ones and let them know how much they mean to you. Listen to their stories, share your own, and build memories that will last beyond the confines of time.

In your pursuit of purpose and fulfillment, don't shy away from the path less traveled. Dare to explore new horizons and allow curiosity to guide you toward uncharted territories. It's in these adventures that we often find the most profound insights and growth.

And as you navigate the complexities of existence, be gentle with yourself. Allow space for imperfections and missteps, for they are essential parts of the journey. Learn from them and let them shape you into a more compassionate and understanding soul.

When you reach the twilight of your days, may you look back with a heart full of gratitude, knowing you lived with intention and embraced every opportunity life offered. Though short, fill your dash with love, laughter, and a kind legacy that inspires future generations.

The clock counts down, relentless and unwavering, pausing for no soul. Tick-tock, tick-tock! And yet, within each tick and tock lies a universe of potential, waiting to be realized. Let the rhythm of time inspire you to seize the day, to act with courage, and to speak with sincerity.

Seek balance in all things, finding harmony between ambition and contentment. Recognize the beauty in the ordinary and celebrate the extraordinary moments when they arise.

As you journey forward, may you carry with you a sense of wonder and an unquenchable thirst for knowledge. Allow the mysteries of life to intrigue you, sparking a desire to learn and grow beyond your present understanding.

Remain true to yourself, honoring your inner voice and values. In a world that often demands conformity, let authenticity be your guiding star. For it is when we are true to ourselves that we bring our best selves to the world.

Remember, you are the author of your own story, and each day presents a blank page awaiting your touch. Write it with intention, passion, and love, creating a narrative that resonates with your deepest aspirations.

The journey is yours to own, and it is magnificent. Embrace it, and may you find joy in the steps you take and the paths you choose.

May blessings accompany you on your journey.

www.ingramcontent.com/pod-product-compliance
Lightning Source LLC
Chambersburg PA
CBHW051345040426
42453CB00007B/424